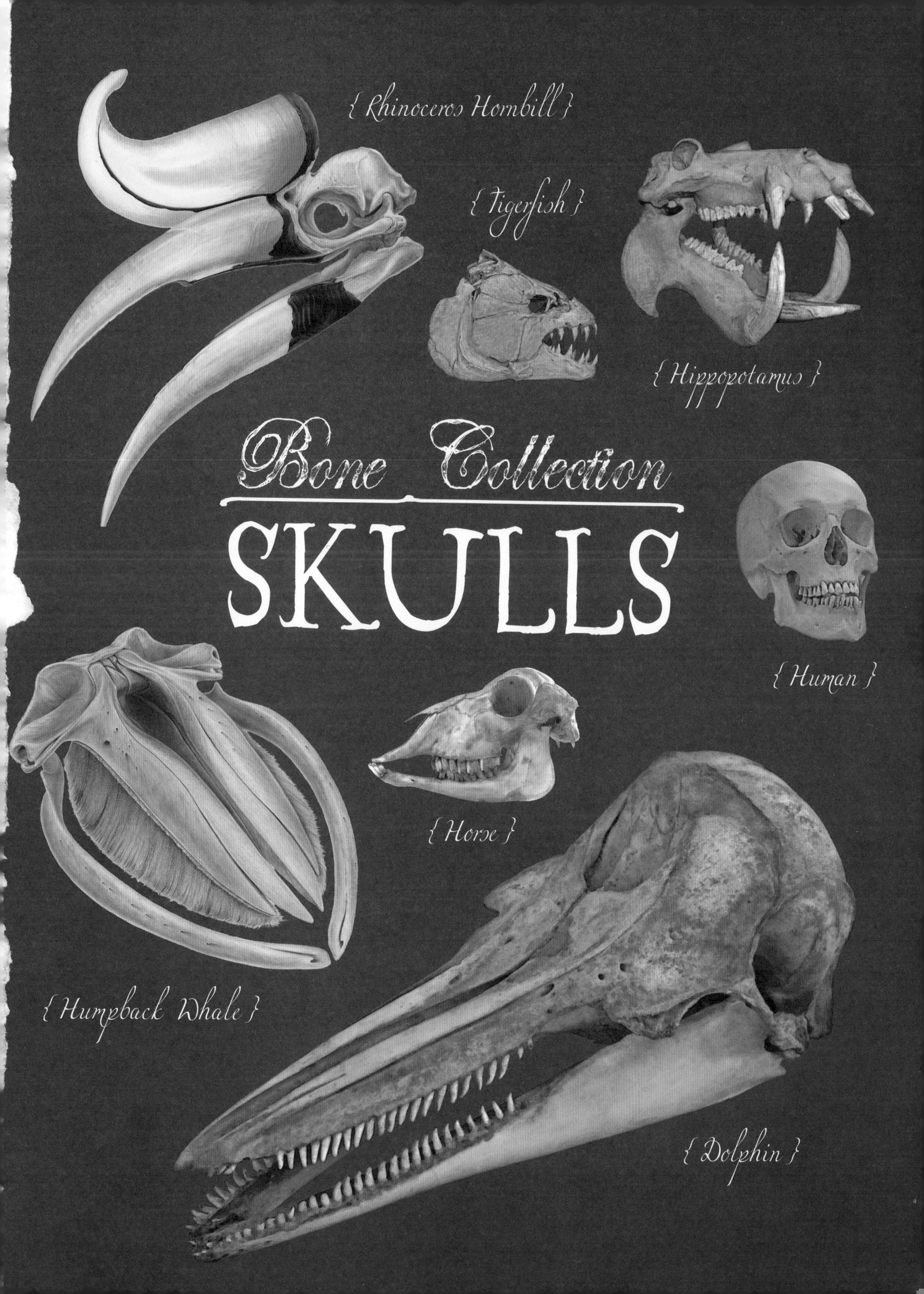

{ Rhinoceros Hornbill }

{ Tigerfish }

{ Hippopotamus }

Bone Collection
SKULLS

{ Human }

{ Humpback Whale }

{ Horse }

{ Dolphin }

Bone Collection

SKULLS

CONTENTS

INTRODUCTION

YOUR HEAD is protected by a shell of tough bone called the skull. This supports and protects some of the most delicate and vital organs inside your body—including most of the sense organs, such as the eyes, ears, and nose, as well as your brain. Although it feels solid, your skull is made up of lots of different bones that fused together in the first couple of years of your life. It only has one movable bone, the jaw, which allows you to chew and speak.

{ Fig 1: Male lion }

{ Fig 2: African elephant }

Animal skulls come in lots of different shapes and sizes. They have adapted to the animals' surroundings and behavior. So a fish may have a long, slim skull to help it swim quickly, while a tiger has huge, powerful jaws so it can crunch through prey.

{ Fig 3: Freshwater crocodile }

SKULL BONES

ANIMALS that have backbones also have skulls to protect their brains and the other delicate organs and tissues of the head. Although one animal's skull may look different from another, the general structure of the skulls themselves is very similar.

TOUGH MATERIAL

Skulls are made of bone, a hard substance that contains proteins, such as collagen, and minerals that help to make it strong. Bone is a living tissue, and it can heal itself when it breaks.

The part that contains the brain is called the braincase.

Exoskeleton

Invertebrates are animals without backbones and skulls. Insects, such as this dragonfly, have a tough skin called an exoskeleton instead. Their limbs and muscles are attached to the exoskeleton.

Some animals' skulls have extra parts sticking out from them, such as sharp beaks or tusks.

SKULL DEVELOPMENT

When a human baby is born, its skull is soft and made up of 44 different parts. The bony parts of a baby's skull are connected by soft areas called fontanelles. As the baby grows, these parts begin to fuse together and become harder.

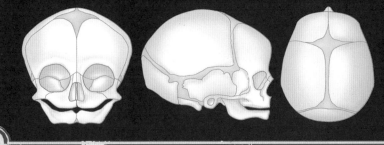

{ Fig 1: Skull development of human infant showing fontanelles in green }

The main part of a skull is made of flat bone. It is called the cranium.

The eye sockets protect and support the eyeballs.

The jawbone, or mandible, is a separate, movable bone that is attached to the cranium by a bony hinge joint and muscles.

HUMPBACK WHALE

BIG EATERS
In one gulp, the humpback can catch thousands of shrimplike plankton called krill.

THE HUMPBACK is a whale that feeds on tiny krill and fish. Its mouth contains plates called baleen, which it uses to filter food from seawater.

BIG HEAD
A humpback's head is about a third of its total body length.

Baleen plates

Ocean wanderers

Humpbacks spend the summer feeding in the Arctic Ocean. In winter, they make a long journey south to warmer waters, where they breed.

Jawbone

Fully grown, the male humpback can reach 46 feet long.

The baleen plates vary in length from 18 inches to 3 feet.

Eye socket

Blowhole for breathing

FILTER FEEDER

A humpback has up to 800 bristlelike baleen plates in its mouth. It gulps water, then forces the water out of its mouth. The plates act like filters, catching tiny animals in the water.

SPY-HOPPER

Sometimes a humpback will stick its head out of the water to look around. This is called spy-hopping.

BALEEN WHALES

THESE ARE large whales that feed on tiny plankton in the water. Baleen whales include humpbacks and the blue whale, which is the biggest animal ever to have lived.

The whale turns as it breaches so that it lands on its back.

LONG-DISTANCE TRAVELER

Gray whales swim across the Pacific Ocean each year. The round trip can be up to 12,000 miles.

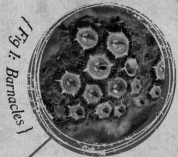

{ Fig 1. Barnacles }

Barnacles grow on the skin of gray whales.

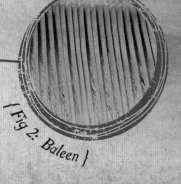

{ Fig 2. Baleen }

Long pectoral fin

The baleen plates are made of keratin, the substance our fingernails are made from.

✂ BIG MOUTH ✂

The bowhead whale has the biggest mouth of any animal, with baleen plates that are 10 feet long. It lives in the Arctic Ocean. To keep warm in the cold Arctic waters, the bowhead's body has a layer of blubber 2 feet thick.

{ Fig 3: Bowhead whale }

BREACHING

Whales sometimes launch themselves out of the water in a display called breaching. No one is sure why they do this. It may be to communicate with other whales, to scare prey, or to rid themselves of itchy parasites on their skin.

Just the tail stays in the water during a humpback's breach.

CALVES

Newborn calves are roughly the length of their mothers' heads. The mothers nurse their calves for about six months.

Bubble net

Humpbacks sometimes fish as a group. They swim in a circle to create a cylinder of bubbles that traps the fish. Then they swim up through the net of bubbles with their mouths open.

DOLPHIN

DOLPHINS are small, toothed whales. They mostly live in the open ocean, where they hunt fish and squid to eat. Dolphins are sociable animals and live in groups called pods.

DOLPHIN SENSES

Dolphins have good eyesight, and their hearing is even better. However, they do not rely on either of these senses to find their prey: they use echolocation instead.

LEAPING

No one knows for sure why dolphins leap out of the water. They might do it to avoid predators, or to get small, biting animals off their skin.

HUNTING

Small, silvery fish often gather together for safety. These groups are called bait balls. Dolphins dive through them to snatch mouthfuls of food.

Most mammals have different types of teeth, but all of a dolphin's teeth are a simple cone shape.

Most dolphins grow to 7–10 feet long.

A dolphin pod may contain just one family, or dozens of families. They communicate with one another using clicks, whistles, and other noises.

A dolphin's braincase is very large, to hold the animal's big brain.

The long bones at the front of the face are often called a beak, or rostrum.

ECHOLOCATION

To echolocate, a dolphin makes sounds called clicks, which bounce off prey and echo back to the dolphin. It uses information from the echo to figure out where the prey is.

Melon head

The dome of a dolphin's head contains an organ called the melon. This is a fluid-filled swelling that the dolphin uses to focus the sounds it makes into sharp clicks.

TOOTHED WHALES

TOOTHED WHALES are ocean predators with powerful bodies for fast swimming. Although they are mammals and breathe in air, many whales can dive and stay underwater for long periods of time.

{ Fig 1: Killer whale teeth }

A sperm whale's skin is often covered with scars from battles with squid and octopuses.

The heavy body can reach 70 feet long and weigh more than 50 tons.

Ruthless hunters

Killer whales are also known as orcas. They are the largest members of the dolphin family, and they hunt in packs. Mothers teach their young how to trap and kill prey.

DIVING DEEP

Sperm whales are the world's largest meat-eaters. They can hold their breath for 90 minutes and dive to incredible depths of up to 10,000 feet to hunt giant squid. At these depths, the weight of water and the lack of light make hunting very difficult.

14

BELUGA

The most obvious feature of beluga whales is their bright white coloring. They live in in the Arctic Ocean, where their white color serves as camouflage against the ice.

{ Fig 2: This beluga whale has blown a small bubble ring. }

WIDESPREAD HUNTERS

These giants live all over the world's oceans. Females and young usually stay in warm waters, while the males travel to cool polar oceans.

The huge head contains the world's biggest brain and special organs that enable sperm whales to communicate and find food in the dark ocean.

LOSING TEETH

A sperm whale's lower jaw contains 20 to 26 pairs of cone-shaped teeth. It's possible that sperm whales don't need their teeth, as many survive without them.

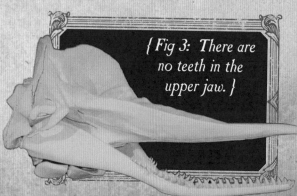

{ Fig 3: There are no teeth in the upper jaw. }

15

CAPYBARA

The eye sockets lead down toward the narrow bones of the snout.

MOST rodents are small animals, but the capybara is as big as a medium-sized dog. It is the largest rodent alive today. These animals live in South America, where they favor watery habitats.

ACTIVE TIMES

Capybaras are active in the evenings and around dawn, when it is cool. They spend the rest of the time resting in their dens or wallowing in water.

Grinding teeth

A capybara has 20 teeth in total. In addition to the four sharp front teeth, there are 16 molars farther back in the jaw to grind food up.

LIVING IN GROUPS

These rodents usually live in groups of up to 20 animals, led by one male. If capybaras sense danger, they bark to one another to raise the alarm.

RAISING YOUNG

Females give birth to up to three babies in their den. The young stay close to the den until they are about four months old.

WATER LIFE

A capybara has webbed feet to help it swim. Its eyes, ears, and nostrils are on top of its head so they stay above water.

The four front teeth are worn down by constant gnawing. They keep growing throughout the animal's life.

The jaws grind food with a forward-backward movement. Unlike most rodent jaws, the capybara's jaw joint does not allow for side-to-side movement.

Adults are about 4 feet long, and the females are usually slightly heavier than males.

17

RODENTS

RODENTS are a group of mammals with large front teeth that they use to gnaw. There are about 2,300 species of rodent. They live in all sorts of habitats, in most parts of the world.

These rodents are agile and fast.

Red squirrels use their long, fluffy tails for balance as they leap and run.

A squirrel's fur can change color throughout the year. It can be any shade of red, brown, gray, or black, but the belly is always white.

Porcupine

A porcupine is a large rodent with long, sharp spines over its body. The spines protect the animal from predators.

FOREST DWELLER

Red squirrels live in the forests of northern Europe and Asia. They are able to survive long, harsh winters by storing food through the summer and fall. Red squirrels mostly feed on seeds.

RATS

These rodents often live alongside humans, eating human food and waste. They can spread disease.

SQUIRREL NEST

This animal's messy nest, or drey, is built from sticks in the fork of a tree. In the spring, up to six young are born. They are called kittens.

CHIPMUNK

Most chipmunks live in woody areas of North America. They feed on seeds and nuts, which they carry in their cheek pouches. During the fall, they gather food to store in their burrows for the long winter.

{ Fig 1: Chipmunks can climb, but they mostly forage on the ground.}

ELEPHANT

THERE are three types of elephant. The African savanna, or bush, elephant is the largest. Weighing up to 7 tons, this animal needs a big, strong skeleton.

{ Fig 1: African elephants have much larger ears than their Asian cousins. }

Living together

Elephants live in groups known as herds. Each herd is run by a female, called the matriarch. Adult males usually live alone or in small groups of their own.

SOCIAL LIFE

Elephants are sociable animals that form very close bonds with one another. They communicate through touch and sound, making low, rumbling calls over long distances.

EXTRA LIMB

An elephant's trunk is its upper lip and nose combined. Controlled by about 100,000 muscles, it is used as a fifth limb that can pull leaves from trees and move them to the mouth, pick up objects, and suck up and spray water or dust.

The long, ivory tusks are incisor teeth. An elephant uses its tusks to strip bark from trees, dig holes in mud, and fight.

The massive skull is strong but light, made of bone that is full of air pockets.

HUGE APPETITES
Adult elephants eat up to 450 pounds of plant matter a day.

Teeth for grinding »

Adults are 13-17 feet tall. Forest elephants are smaller than savanna elephants.

The lower jaw moves forward and backward as the elephant grinds its food—unlike cows, which chew grass using side-to-side motions.

TUSKED ANIMALS

A TUSK is a long, pointed tooth that usually keeps growing throughout an animal's life. It can be used for fighting or digging, or for moving around.

BABIRUSA

This strange Indonesian mammal has a set of piglike tusks, and another set of tusks that look like deer horns.

FIGHTING WALRUSES

Male walruses can be twice the size of female walruses. They use their great size to fight each other, and they can do serious damage with their long tusks.

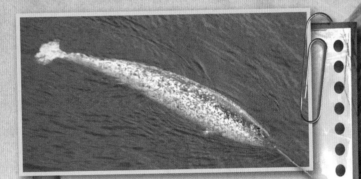

Narwhal

Narwhals are small whales. The males have one long, straight tusk, measuring up to 10 feet long. Occasionally, a narwhal may grow two tusks. The females have much shorter tusks.

WARTHOG

Warthogs have two large tusks that cur[ve]
up and out of their upper jaws. These [tusks]
can grow up to 26 inches long in ma[les,]
10 inches in females. A second, s[maller]
pair of tusks grows from the lo[wer]

{ Fig 1: Warthogs are found throughout Africa, south of the Sahara. }

LAND OR SEA

Walruses come onto the land to mate and have their young, but they hunt for food underwater. These marine mammals eat shellfish, sea worms, and slow-swimming fish they find on the seabed. They use their tusks to haul themselves back up onto land or ice.

A walrus's skin is gray with pink markings, especially when the animal has been in the sun.

Males' tusks can be over 3 feet long!

The thick neck has layers of blubbery fat that provide protection when males fight.

HORSE

HORSES BELONG to a group of animals called equids. They have stocky, strong bodies supported by four long, powerful legs, and they are fast runners. Members of the horse family usually live in groups called herds.

This bone forms the [...] of the nose. In a living animal, the rest of the nose is supported by cartilage.

The mandible (jawbone) is long and deep. It is attached to the skull by a joint that allows the horse to grind tough grass between the teeth at the back of the jaw.

Incisors at the front for cropping grass

Mustangs

These North American horses are descendants of horses brought over by the Spanish hundreds of years ago.

GRAZERS

All members of the equid family eat grass, as well as some other plants. Grass is very difficult to digest, so equids have to eat a lot to get enough nutrients from their diet.

The orbit (the bone cavity for the eyeball) is high up on the skull, so the horse can watch out for predators.

STALLIONS

A herd of horses usually has a male leader, or stallion, and a group of females, or mares. Stallions can be very aggressive. Their main weapon is a strong kick.

PRZEWALSKI'S HORSE

There is only one remaining species of wild horse: the Przewalski. They live on grasslands in Mongolia, and are named after a Russian scientist who studied them.

Horses are 7–8 feet long and up to 6 feet tall at the shoulder.

25

HERD ANIMALS

MANY animals that graze on grass live in social groups called herds. Grazing is time-consuming, and it leaves animals exposed to predators on open plains without trees to hide behind.

MIGRATION

Wildebeest, or gnu, are African herding antelopes. Some wildebeest migrate, which means that they go on long journeys to find better grazing conditions.

The shoulders are tall and packed with muscles so the wildebeest can escape from cheetahs and lions.

Bison

American bison are enormous animals that can weigh as much as a rhinoceros. There were once at least 50 million bison on the American grasslands, before hunting left them close to extinction.

ZEBRA

Scientists believe the zebra's stripes may make it hard for predators to identify a single prey in a running herd. Stripes are particularly effective in hiding foals.

This is a black wildebeest. It has a dark body, a stiff upright mane, and a white tail-tip.

A wildebeest's horns are used for defense and fighting. In males, they can grow up to 3 feet.

FEEDING

Wildebeest migrations are determined by rainfall and the availability of grass, but also by the location of minerals, such as phosphorus and nitrogen, which these antelopes need in their diet.

LECHWE

Lechwe are antelopes that gather in large herds of thousands of animals. They live around flooded plains in southern Africa. Lechwe can run very quickly through water, and this keeps them safe from predators.

{ Fig 1: Red lechwe run through flooded grassland in the Okavango Delta in Africa. }

27

TIGER

THE TIGER IS the largest, most powerful member of the cat family. It is a supreme predator that combines speed, strength, and stealth to find and kill its prey.

QUICK LEARNERS

Tigers usually live and hunt alone, although cubs live with their mothers while they learn how to hunt.

These canine teeth are dagger-shaped and can grow to be 4 inches long.

These slicing teeth on the side of the tiger's mouth are called carnassial teeth.

Sumatran tiger

The Sumatran tiger is the rarest of all tigers. There are believed to be fewer than 400 of them left alive in the wild.

Adult tigers are up to 10 feet long. The largest is the Siberian tiger.

TIGER STRIPES
The stripes help a tiger hide from its prey in the dappled shadows of a forest. No two tigers have the same stripe pattern.

The jaws are very flexible so the predator can open its mouth wide to hold on to large prey.

UNDER THREAT
Tigers live in forests and mountains in southern and eastern Asia. A century ago, there were six types of tiger, but three have become extinct.

SIBERIAN TIGER
Siberian tigers have longer, thicker coats than cousins that live in warmer places. Finding prey is harder when the ground is covered in snow.

BIG CATS

ALL cats are skilled hunters. They react quickly, move swiftly and quietly, and are equipped with incredible senses and powerful jaws and paws.

FAST HUNTERS

Cheetahs hunt on large expanses of African grasslands, where they rely mostly on their sense of sight to find and follow antelopes. Cheetahs are the fastest land mammals. They can reach 65 miles per hour over short distances.

The orbits (eye sockets) face forward, giving the cat excellent vision.

Snow leopard

Snow leopards have small ears, broad paws, and thick fluffy hair to help them survive in their cold mountain habitat. Little is known about these shy predators.

PUMA

Two big cats live in the Americas: jaguars and pumas. Jaguars are the third-largest cats after tigers and lions. They have fawn-colored fur with dark patches. Pumas are usually sandy colored, and they are also known as mountain lions or cougars.

{ Fig 1: In parts of the southeastern U.S.A., pumas are known as Florida panthers. }

CHOKE HOLD

Once a cheetah has its prey within reach, it leaps and grips with claws and jaws. It sinks its teeth into the victim's windpipe, cutting off its air supply so death comes quickly.

The long tail is used to balance the cheetah as it chases prey.

SOCIAL HUNTER

The majority of lions live in Africa, although there is a small population of Asian lions in India. Most cats live alone, but lions prefer to live in social groups called prides.

BIGHORN SHEEP

BIGHORN SHEEP are wild sheep that live in a range of habitats from mountains to dry deserts. They belong to the bovid family, which includes cattle and antelopes.

This is the skull of a male, or ram. The tough bone is strong enough to withstand powerful blows from another ram.

Separate groups

Bighorn sheep live in social groups, with males in one group and females with their young in another.

RUTTING

At mating time, male bighorn sheep fight each other, clashing their horns and head-butting. A fight, or rut, can last for several hours.

BUTTING HEADS

Males fight by rearing up on their hind legs before turning, leaping, or walking away. Eventually, they run at each other and head-butt with great force.

MIGRATING

During the summer, bighorn sheep move toward higher ground. They are nimble climbers. In the winter, they move back to lower areas.

The horns are wrapped around bone that grows out of the skull.

Unlike deer, a sheep's horns do not fall off after mating season.

HEAVY HORNS

A bighorn's horns can weigh 30 pounds—more than the rest of a male's skeleton.

Adults are up to 6 feet long. Males are bigger than females and up to twice their weight.

GRAZING ANIMALS

GRAZING animals live on a diet of tough grass. They have special guts to digest nutrients from this diet, often bringing up food from their stomachs to chew a second time.

Northern grazers

Red deer live in warm and cool northern countries. Females are called hinds, and they live in groups that are led by one hind. Males live in separate groups.

Male Cape buffaloes are larger and heavier than the females, but they both have two curving horns.

COOL GRAZERS

Cape buffaloes live in big herds that can survive in a range of habitats, but they always stay close to a source of freshwater. They mostly graze after the sun has gone down, when the air is cooler.

The horns meet in the center of the animal's skull, creating a raised area called a boss.

GIRAFFE

Giraffe skulls have large, hornlike prominences called ossicones. Males use these to fight each other.

SAFETY IN NUMBERS

A buffalo herd often moves and feeds together. Staying in a big group protects them from predators such as lions, leopards, and African hunting dogs.

✤ LLAMA ✤

Llamas, vicunas, and guanacos are slender-legged grazing animals of South America. They belong to the same family as camels. Humans have bred llamas for their wool and meat, and to carry loads.

{ Fig 1: Llamas have woolly fur that keeps them warm in mountain pastures. }

POLAR BEAR

POLAR BEARS are fearless predators that are able to survive in the frozen Arctic. There is little land around, but polar bears are just as comfortable on ice sheets and in the water.

There is a large gap between the front teeth and the carnassial teeth at the back.

Keeping warm

Although polar bears appear white or creamy-yellow, the skin under their fur is actually black. Each hair is hollow, which probably helps the bear keep warm and swim.

RAISING YOUNG

Female polar bears dig dens in deep drifts of snow and give birth to their cubs during the winter. The new family emerges in spring. The cubs stay with their mother for about two years.

The skull bones join at the top of the head at the sagittal crest.

SWIMMING

Polar bears use their paddlelike paws to swim. They can travel many miles through the Arctic's icy waters.

MEAT-EATER

There are almost no plants in the cold north, but polar bears rely on a diet of meat. Their favorite prey is seal, but they will attack almost any animal.

Adults are up to 11 ½ feet long. Males can weigh twice as much as females.

LETHAL BITE

Polar bears use their powerful jaws to bite the necks of prey such as seals.

BEARS

MOST members of the bear family have huge, bulky bodies and powerful limbs with long, sharp claws. They have black, brown, or white fur, and the males are bigger than females.

A brown bear's jaws are strong enough to bite through metal.

SLOTH BEAR

Shaggy-haired sloth bears live in parts of Southeast Asia. These rarely seen bears eat berries, honey, and insects, and they are mostly nocturnal.

The hind legs are short. Although a bear can run fast, it usually relies on strength rather than speed.

Bear family

Brown bears often spend the winter in hibernation, or deep sleep. Female brown bears can give birth to up to four cubs while they are safe in their dens.

{ Fig 1: Brown bear claws }

GIANT PANDA

There are few panda bears left in the wild. They live in the bamboo forests of central China, and feed almost solely on bamboo. Loss of habitat has greatly affected their chances of survival as a species.

{ Fig 2: Pandas are easily recognized by their black and white fur. }

The muscular front legs can kill another animal with a single swipe. All four paws are armed with long, sharp claws.

BIG NOSES

Bears have an incredible sense of smell, but their eyesight and hearing are less well-developed. Their snouts are large, but their eyes are small.

SUN BEAR

The smallest bears live in Southeast Asia. They climb trees to find food and build nests. They are called sun bears after the patches of golden fur on their chests.

GRIZZLY BEARS

American brown bears are often called grizzlies because the tips of their fur lighten with age, giving them a grizzled appearance. Brown bears eat berries, nuts, small mammals, and insects. Some brown bears also wade into rivers to catch fish.

HIPPOPOTAMUS

THE word hippopotamus means "river horse." These large animals spend much of their time in rivers and lakes, but they are more closely related to whales than horses.

KEEPING COOL

Hippos spend large amounts of time in water to keep cool. Their nostrils and eyes are at the top of their heads so they can breathe and see even when the head is mostly submerged.

Big mouth

A hippo shows its massive teeth to threaten attackers or other hippos. The male's canine teeth, or tusks, grow to 18 inches long.

Canine teeth

The jaw hinge is far back on the skull so the hippo can open its mouth wide.

PYGMY HIPPO

The small pygmy hippo lives in forests in western parts of Africa. Some populations are very close to extinction because their habitat has been destroyed.

The nostrils and small orbits (eyeholes) are at the top of the skull.

Molar teeth

The canine teeth, or tusks, are not used for eating. Instead, grass is clipped with thick lips, and then chewed by the molar teeth.

WALKING

Hippos have large, barrel-shaped bodies and short legs. They are better at swimming than walking.

Adults hippos grow up to 12 feet long.

AQUATIC MAMMALS

The head is large, with small eyes and ear openings.

WHILE most mammals live on land, a number of them returned to a watery life a long time ago. Their bodies have adapted to this different habitat, and their limbs are usually small or flipperlike.

Otters

Otters are aquatic animals with long, slender bodies and thick fur. Most otter species live in rivers, but sea otters make their home in the Pacific Ocean.

The skin of a manatee is mostly hairless and gray. There are bristles around the snout.

TAKE A BREATH

Like all aquatic mammals, manatees must return to the water's surface to breathe. They can hold their breath underwater, but only for three to four minutes at a time when active.

DUGONG

Dugongs are sometimes called sea cows or cow pigs. They belong to the same group of animals as manatees—the sirenians. There are three species of manatee, but only one type of dugong.

{ Fig I: Dugongs live in coastal areas from the southwest Pacific Ocean to the African coast of the Indian Ocean. }

MOVING TEETH

Manatees have one very unusual feature in their skulls. As they age, their molar teeth move toward the front of the mouth, and new molars grow at the back of their jaws. This means that a manatee gets replacement teeth throughout its life, like a shark!

The body is large and heavy.

The forelimbs are flippers.

Instead of hind limbs, the paddle-shaped tail beats up and down to propel the manatee through the water.

SEA LION

A sea lion can stay underwater for ten minutes at a time. It slows down its heart rate so it needs less oxygen when it dives deep.

SPOTTED HYENA

HYENAS are intelligent, social carnivores that live in Africa and parts of western Asia. Spotted hyenas live in family groups led by females. They communicate by whooping and cackling.

HUNTING

Spotted hyenas scavenge food, but they are also superb hunters. They can run far and fast, chasing prey until it gives up.

The massive teeth and jaws can crunch with such force that even large bones are crushed.

Strong body

A hyena has a slim body and face, but its forelimbs are longer and more muscular than its hind legs, giving it a strange, sloping body.

EATING BONES

A hyena's stomach contains a very high level of hydrochloric acid, which is strong enough to break down bone.

PACK HUNTERS

By hunting as a pack, hyenas are able to target large prey, including zebras, but they mostly attack antelope and wildebeest young.

This large area at the back of the skull is where the powerful jaw muscles attach.

TIGHT GRIP

Members of the hyena family have short jaws, which allow them to grip tightly onto their prey. They have fewer teeth than other carnivores (except cats), but their teeth are very big.

This animal has one of the strongest bites in the animal kingdom.

Adults are up to 4 ½ feet long. Females are bigger than males.

HYENAS AND CANIDS

HYENAS live similar lives to many members of the dog (canid) family, even though they are more closely related to other carnivores, such as cats and civets.

All hyenas have long, dark stripes of fur down their backs.

Jackal

There are three species, or types, of jackal: golden jackals, side-striped jackals, and black-backed jackals. They are all canids and live in Africa, parts of Europe, and southern Asia.

FAMILY MEMBERS

Although striped hyenas usually live alone, they may gather in clans at breeding times.

GOOD SMELLERS

Like members of the dog family, hyenas have a good sense of smell. They use this to find prey or carrion (dead animals), but they also use it to identify their territory.

Hyenas can raise the fur on their backs to make themselves appear bigger.

AFRICAN WILD DOG
African wild, or hunting, dogs live in complex social groups. Normally, just one pair of dogs has young, and other members of the group help to raise the pups.

A striped hyena is about 4 ½ feet long, which is shorter than a spotted hyena.

GRAY WOLF

Gray wolves are the largest members of the canid family. They once roamed across large areas of Europe and Asia. However, because of habitat loss and hunting, there are now far fewer of them.

{ Fig 1: Gray wolves hunt alone or as a pack. They are the ancestors of all domestic dogs. }

47

HUMAN

HUMANS HAVE similar skulls to chimps, gorillas, and orangutans. They all have flat faces with well-developed jaws and large orbits to hold two forward-facing eyes.

BIG BRAINS

The scientific name for modern humans is *Homo sapiens*, which means "wise man." Humans have big brains, live in complex social groups, and make tools.

The braincase is large and rounded to make room for a human's big brain.

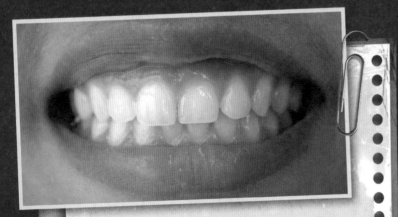

Teeth

An adult's mouth contains 28-32 teeth that allow humans to eat a wide range of food. Animals that eat many types of food are called omnivores.

Human jaws are small but extremely powerful, and the muscles allow an incredible range of movement that enables speech.

CLEAR VISION

Human brains have enlarged areas for language, thought, and learning new things. An area at the back of the brain is called the occipital lobe. This is where information from the eyes is turned into vision.

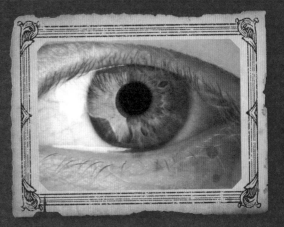

The eyes face forward, giving us excellent sight. Humans can see distance and color and can calculate how far away something is.

Humans have flat faces with no snouts. The nose is constructed from cartilage, which we cannot see in a bony skull.

DELICATE OPERATIONS

Humans are able to carry out complicated actions, such as delicate surgery. This is because we can learn, understand, and communicate with one another, as well as make and use tools.

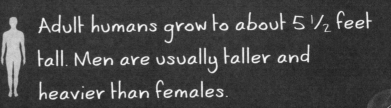

Adult humans grow to about 5 ½ feet tall. Men are usually taller and heavier than females.

APES AND MONKEYS

APES AND MONKEYS are furry animals that usually live in family groups. They have grasping hands, and most of them live in trees. There are about 380 types of monkey and ape. They belong to a group of mammals called primates.

Chimpanzee

Chimpanzees are humans' closest relatives. They live in family groups and communicate with one another using complex sounds, such as "pant-hoots." They can also use tools.

LONG JUMPER

A tarsier has very long limbs and is able to leap between trees, reaching out to grab onto distant branches. It hunts for insects at night.

Tarsiers find prey using their large eyes and ears.

A tarsier's head can swivel 180 degrees so the primate can look behind itself.

The total length of head and body is about 6 ½ inches, and the tail is even longer.

MANDRILL

Most mammals have dull-looking fur in shades of brown or black, but male mandrills are very colorful. Not only do they have colorful faces, they also have blue bottoms!

The long fingers and toes can grip tightly onto slender branches.

HOWLER MONKEY

It is easier to hear a howler monkey than it is to see one. These monkeys live in the tall trees of a rain forest, out of sight. Their calls, however, are extremely loud and can be heard up to 3 miles away.

{ Fig 1: A howler monkey howls to tell other monkeys to stay out of its family's territory. }

DUCK-BILLED PLATYPUS

The front of the skull extends to make a long bill or beak shape.

AT first, no one knew what type of animal a duck-billed platypus was. Now scientists classify them as a special type of mammal called monotremes (mammals that lay eggs). They get their name from the ducklike bill on their heads.

Blind swimmer

Underwater, the platypus closes its eyes, ears, and nostrils. Its smooth shape, sleek fur, paddlelike tail, and webbed feet make it a good swimmer.

A platypus's fur is very dense and waterproof.

EGG LAYERS

Although duck-billed platypuses feed their young on milk like all other mammals, they do not give birth to them. They lay eggs instead.

THE BILL
Underwater, the platypus uses its bill to feel its way and to pick up electrical signals its prey gives off.

RIVER HUNTERS
Platypuses live in eastern Australia. They hunt freshwater shrimps and other small animals, especially the larvae of flies and beetles.

VENOMOUS SPUR
Male platypuses have small, sharp spurs on their hind ankles. Each spur is hollow and is connected to a venom gland in the thigh. The spurs are used against rival males.

The bill measures 2-3 inches long.

Adults are up to 2 feet long, and the males are slightly larger than the females.

Young platypuses have molar teeth that they lose as they mature. This is an adult's skull.

MONOTREMES AND MARSUPIALS

WHILE MONOTREMES lay eggs, marsupials are a type of mammal that give birth but keep their young in a pouch. The young animal feeds on its mother's milk as it grows in the pouch.

A young koala leaves its mother's pouch when it is about five months old.

KOALAS

Koalas are marsupials. They give birth to a single baby that weighs only one fiftieth of an ounce when it climbs into its mother's pouch.

A koala's body is bearlike in shape, and there is no tail. The fur is extremely thick.

TASMANIAN DEVIL

The teeth of a Tasmanian devil, a meat-eating marsupial, are similar to those of cats and dogs. A Tasmanian devil kills prey by using a powerful crushing bite, although they mostly scavenge for food.

{ Fig 1: A Tasmanian devil can crush a skull and most other large bones in its massive jaws. }

TOUGH FOOD

Koalas eat a diet of eucalyptus leaves. They chew the leaves into a paste, but it is still difficult to digest, so koalas have very long intestines.

Big face, tiny brain

A marsupial skull, such as this water opossum, generally has a large face area and a small braincase. There is usually a sagittal crest on top of the skull, where the muscles that close the jaws are fixed.

A koala climbs by gripping on to a branch with its clawed feet and pulling forward.

SHORT-BEAKED ECHIDNA

Echidnas are monotremes. The echidna's mouth is at the end of a long, slender snout. It uses its long tongue to catch tiny bugs or worms.

RHINOCEROS HORNBILL

LOUD, large, and brightly colored, the rhinoceros hornbill is hard to miss. It takes its name from the huge crest on its beak, which is curved in the shape of a rhino's horn.

Hollow crest

The crest is colored bright orange and yellow.

Eye socket

BONY BEAK

Just as our skulls include our teeth, the skulls of birds include their beaks, or bills. The beaks are made from a bony inner structure covered by a layer of hard keratin.

SOUND CHAMBER

The crest is lightweight and hollow. It works in the same way as the body of a guitar, making the sound of the bird's calls much louder.

Forest bird

Rhinoceros hornbills live in tropical forests. Their bright colors and loud calls help them communicate through the trees.

LONG BILL

The hornbill's long bill is a very useful tool. The bird uses it to pick fruit and grab at small animals in the trees.

Bill curves downward.

Lower jaw

The rhinoceros hornbill is about the same size as a swan, measuring 40 inches long.

HORNBILLS

THESE unmistakable birds have long, sensitive beaks, and many also have large crests. They are omnivores, which means that they eat both plants and animals.

Red crest

{ Fig 1: Eyelashes }

A hornbill has eyelashes made from modified feathers. These lashes help shade the eyes from bright sunlight.

SULAWESI RED-KNOBBED HORNBIRD

PREENING

Hornbills use their long bills to keep their feathers clean and tidy, an activity known as preening.

Long tail feathers

LONG LIVES

Hornbills are some of the longest-living birds in the world. They can survive for up to 70 years.

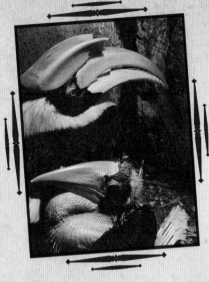

HORNBILL CHICK

This Indian hornbill chick does not yet have a crest on its bill like its parent. The crest will take five years to develop fully.

Taking to the air

The African gray hornbill has broad, rounded wings. It makes a lot of noise when it flies, so in dense forests you're likely to hear it before you see it.

SEALED NEST

When the female is ready to lay her eggs, she climbs into a nest in a hollow tree and seals the entrance with mud. The male feeds mother and chicks through a small slit until the chicks are big enough to break out. Then both parents feed the chicks.

GROWING UP

Young hornbills stay with their parents for six months after leaving the nest.

GROUND BIRD

Most hornbills fly, but ground hornbills stay on the ground, where they hunt frogs, snails, reptiles, and small mammals. They live in family groups of between five and 10 birds. Each group controls its own territory, which may be as large as 40 square miles.

{ Fig 2: Southern ground hornbill }

FLAMINGO

The braincase is small compared to the huge beak.

THERE are six different types of flamingo, but they all look similar—long, spindly legs; colorful feathers; a long, elegant neck; and an oddly shaped beak.

SALTY LAKES

Flamingos feed on tiny shrimps and other small animals, or on algae, in lakes. They are often found in alkaline, or very salty, lakes.

Skim feeder

When it feeds, a flamingo dips its bill upside down in the water so it can skim food from near the surface. Large flamingos feed on small animals, but smaller ones often feed on algae.

FILTERING

A flamingo's bill has little rows of hairy plates, called lamellae, on the inside edges. These work like a sieve, so when the bird sucks in water, animals are caught on the lamellae, and then swallowed.

Flamingos can grow up to 5 feet tall. They have very long, featherless legs and large, webbed feet.

LONG LEGS

Flamingos are graceful flyers, although their bodies are so big it takes them some effort to take off. When standing in water, they often balance on just one leg.

Underneath the hornlike outer layer of the beak are these bony parts, which provide strength and support.

BRIGHT PINK

Most flamingos have coral-pink, red, or white feathers. The colors come from the food they eat, in particular little pink crustaceans (small, shelled animals). The pigment (color) is stored in the bird's feathers, but it fades in strong sunlight.

The beak looks heavy, but its insides are made of a light, spongy bone that is full of air.

BIRDS

BIRDS have feathers and lay eggs, and most of them can fly. They inhabit most parts of the world, even cold polar regions. There are about 10,200 types of bird, and they vary in size from tiny hummingbirds to tall, flightless ostriches.

The casque is a helmetlike structure on the cassowary's head. It is covered with keratin, the same material that is found in a bird's beak and feathers.

The cassowary's skin is brightly colored around the head and long neck.

Living on the water

Ducks, geese, and swans are known as waterfowl. They usually live around freshwater, and in places where rivers flow into the sea. Waterfowl have plump bodies and waterproof feathers.

FLIGHTLESS BIRDS

There are three types of cassowary, and they live in rain forests in parts of Australia, New Guinea, and other surrounding islands. They are the world's second-heaviest bird, after the ostrich. Like the ostrich and emu, they cannot fly.

The body is covered in a thick layer of black, glossy feathers.

WADERS

Wading birds live along coasts, feeding on animals in or near the water. Many waders, such as this avocet, have long, slender legs for walking in the shallows. They tend to form large flocks.

BIG HEAD, BIG KICK

The casque may help cassowaries make their deep, booming calls. These birds are among the world's most dangerous because they have a powerful kick and a long, daggerlike claw on one of their toes.

MACAW

Parrots are brightly colored, intelligent birds that live in warm countries, often in tropical forests. They have strong, hooked, flexible beaks for prizing open nuts, and they use their feet to hold on to their food as they nibble it.

The loose skin on the bird's neck is called a wattle. It changes color to show the bird's mood.

CORMORANT

Cormorants dive into water, swimming beneath the surface to depths of 100 feet or more. Their strong legs and webbed feet help them chase fish through the water.

{ Fig 1: Cormorants hold their wings out to dry between dives. }

63

BALD EAGLE

BALD EAGLES are large birds of prey that live in North America. They have huge beaks and clawlike talons, which they use to grab other animals and tear them into chunks they can swallow.

These birds have a wingspan of up to 8 feet.

The large, hooked beak pierces and rips through meat.

CHICKS

Females usually lay up to three eggs at a time. The eggs take about 35 days to hatch. Both parents care for their young.

Adult colors

Bald eagles begin to develop yellow eyes and white heads and tails during their third year. Their name comes from an old word meaning "white headed."

COLORATION

Young bald eagles are dark brown all over, including their eyes and beaks. As they age, their colors begin to change.

SOARING

These birds sometimes go on long migrations to find food. They soar through the sky using air currents, beating their wings slowly.

HUNTING FISH

Bald eagles prefer to hunt fish. They perch near water, watching carefully before they attack. Then they swoop down to grab a fish with their talons, and return to the perch to eat it.

The orbits (eyeholes) are very large in birds of prey.

IN FLIGHT

Bald eagles fly most in the summer, when the winds are good and there is less rain.

BIRDS OF PREY

BIRDS that hunt other animals need size, speed, superb eyesight, and powerful beaks and talons. Birds of prey usually seek out their victims from the sky, or from a high perch.

KITES

Brahminy kites are also called white-headed fish eagles. Although they do hunt fish and other animals, these birds also scavenge, which means they eat any dead animals they can find.

VULTURE

Vultures are birds of prey that mostly feed on animal carcasses (dead bodies) they find.

KEEN EYESIGHT

A bird of prey's eyes face forward so it can focus on even very small objects. It can work out exactly how far away a victim is before it dives in for the kill.

Long wing feathers stretch out like fingers, helping the bird to almost float in the air.

A Brahminy kite has a wingspan (measured from the tip of one outstretched wing to the other) of about 4 feet.

BARN OWL

Owls are nocturnal birds of prey. They have large, front-facing eyes to help them see in the dark. They also have incredible hearing.

RAPTOR SKULL

A secretary bird's skull is very similar to the skull of an eagle, which is another type of large raptor.

STAMPING

Secretary birds live on the African grasslands. Although they can fly, these birds mostly walk through the grass, looking for snakes or other prey. When a secretary bird finds an animal to eat, it stamps on it to kill it.

{ Fig 1: Secretary bird }

GABOON VIPER

GABOON VIPERS

lie among fallen leaves
and wait for small
animals to pass by.
They strike with speed,
injecting deadly venom
into their prey's flesh.

The huge fangs are hinged, so
they can swing forward when the
snake wants to bite.

Even though the
viper has a series of
fangs, only one pair
is used at a time.
These other fangs
are ready to replace
the front pair when
they wear out or
fall out.

The fangs
are up to
2 inches long.

Because the lower
jaws are not attached
at the front, each
jaw can move
independently
of the other.

SLIDING ALONG

Gaboon vipers have massive bodies.
The larger ones do not slither from
side to side, but move along in a
straight line, like giant caterpillars!

DEADLY VENOM

Vipers have large venom glands behind their eyes. Their venom usually breaks down blood cells, so the victim bleeds to death slowly.

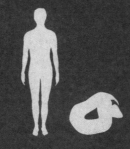

Gaboon vipers are 5 feet long, making them the largest vipers in the world.

The jawbones are long and lightweight and can open wide.

Skin shedding

As snakes grow, their skin does not grow with them. When the old skin becomes too tight, they must shed it, revealing a soft new skin underneath. This is called molting, or ecdysis.

HORNED SNAKE

Gaboon vipers have two small horns located in between their nostrils. Scientists don't know what these horns are used for.

SHARP TEETH

The snake's venom enters each fang through a small hole at the top and leaves from a hole near the tooth's bottom. Every two months, new fangs replace the old ones.

SNAKES

In this position, a cobra is ready to strike.

SNAKES are reptiles with extremely long bodies, small heads, and no limbs. They have up to 400 vertebrae (bones of the spine) that move easily, so a snake can slither and crawl.

SQUEEZING PREY

Pythons and boas do not kill their prey with venom. They wrap their coils around a victim and squeeze it to death.

This forest cobra is one of the largest cobra species in the world.

AGGRESSIVE COBRAS

A forest cobra's venom can kill a person in less than two hours. Cobras are often aggressive snakes. If they are scared, they will attack rather than slither away. They hunt small animals, such as lizards and birds.

When a cobra wants to scare another animal away, it raises its body and stretches the ribs near its head to make a hood.

Green tree python

Green tree python

Green tree pythons coil themselves around the branch of a tree and keep an eye open for prey. They are able to sense movement, and they can detect the heat made by another animal's body.

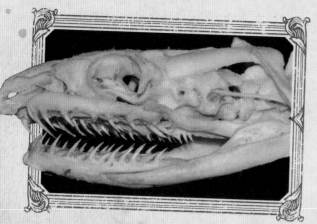

PLENTY OF TEETH

Most snakes belong to a group called the colubrids. Many colubrids do not have venom, but they do have plenty of daggerlike teeth, like this mole snake.

LIVE BIRTH OR EGGS

Cobras belong to a group of snakes called the elapids. They are all venomous and live in warm places, especially forests and grasslands. Most elapids lay eggs, although many other types of snake give birth to their young.

A tree python lies coiled on a branch waiting for passing prey.

❦ SPITTING ❦

Some cobras are able to spit their venom through small holes in their fangs. They have an extraordinary ability to aim at an attacker's eyes. The venom causes pain and even blindness.

{ Fig 1: You need to stand back at least 10 feet from a spitting cobra to avoid being sprayed with venom. }

CROCODILE

THE largest reptiles belong to the crocodilian family, which includes crocodiles, alligators, caimans, and gharials. They all have flat bodies, huge jaws, and a predatory way of life.

WATERY LIFESTYLE

Some crocodiles live in salty water, while others prefer rivers and lakes. They must return to land to lay their eggs and take care of their young.

The four lower teeth stick out on either side of the crocodile's upper jaw.

Gentle touch

Female crocodiles are caring mothers, protecting their nest of eggs while the babies grow inside. They help their young to hatch and even carry them gently in their jaws.

A crocodile's snout is longer and thinner than the snout of an alligator.

FEARLESS HUNTER

The Australian freshwater crocodile is a fearless beast that preys on fish, but it will attack anything, including birds, reptiles, and mammals.

OPEN WIDE

Crocodiles have a powerful bite. They cannot chew, so they swallow small prey whole. They break larger prey into pieces by thrashing and spinning underwater as they grip it in their jaws.

The orbits are situated at the top of the skull so a crocodile can see above water while most of its body and head are submerged.

AMBUSH

Crocodiles lie by the water's edge, waiting for prey to approach before pouncing and dragging their victim underwater.

Australia's saltwater crocodiles can grow up to 27 feet long.

REPTILES

SNAKES, crocodiles, turtles, and lizards are all types of reptile. These animals mostly lay eggs, have tough, scaly skin, and are mostly cold-blooded.

The slender head narrows toward the front, and the eyes are large.

Spectacled caiman

Spectacled caimans are similar to alligators. They live in Central and South America. Like other members of the crocodile family, caimans are killed for their attractive skins.

Hawksbill turtles measure up to 4 feet long.

TORTOISE

Tortoises live on land and use their shells to protect themselves from predators. This is a hinged tortoise, which can shut itself inside its shell completely.

GHARIAL

Indian gharials are critically endangered. There are fewer than 200 adults alive in the wild today. These reptiles have very long, slender snouts and grow to 23 feet long.

{ Fig 1: A gharial resting underwater }

The front limbs are adapted for gentle swimming. There is a claw on each flipper.

The upper shell, or carapace, has a beautiful pattern, while the lower shell is white.

REEF HUNTERS

Hawksbill turtles live in the shallow water around coral reefs, where they search for small animals like sponges, shellfish, and jellyfish to eat.

TUATARA

Tuataras are found only on small islands near New Zealand, where they live in burrows.

GILA MONSTER

GILA MONSTERS are venomous reptiles that live in hot, dry places in the southwestern United States. These predators spend the coldest days and nights asleep in their burrows. They are able to store food as fat inside their tails.

DANGEROUS BITE

Few lizards are venomous, but Gila monsters produce venom in the glands of their lower jaws. They mostly hunt by smell, and they can survive for weeks without eating. When they do eat, Gilas can consume huge amounts—up to half a third body weight at a time.

Ancient skin

Gila monsters have beadlike scales similar to those seen on dinosaur fossils.

The heavy, broad skull is covered with lumps called epidermal knobs.

The long, sharp teeth are ideal for a predator that hunts fast-moving animals.

DEFENSIVE POSE

Gila monsters are not fast movers, so they rely on hissing and other methods to deter enemies. Their bold colors warn that they have a venomous bite.

BLUE TONGUE

Many reptiles sense smells by flicking their tongues to trap tiny scent particles. The tongue then touches a special place on the roof of the mouth, where it tastes the particles.

Curved teeth

Gila monsters are up to 2 feet long. They have stocky bodies, large heads, and short, fat tails.

KILLING PREY

When a Gila monster has found its prey, it sinks its sharp teeth into the victim's flesh and holds on tightly with the claws of its front feet.

LIZARDS

LIZARDS are reptiles that lay eggs and have scaly skin, a long tail, and four limbs. There are at least 5,000 species of lizard, and they are more common in warm countries than cool ones. The smallest lizard would fit on a fingertip, but the largest ones are heavier than an adult human.

The casque is a tough, helmetlike crest that extends over the lizard's neck. Males have larger casques than females.

Scary display

When a frilled lizard is scared, it raises its huge umbrellalike cloak of skin and hisses loudly. After this impressive display, the lizard runs up a tree for extra safety.

ALL CHANGE

A chameleon's skin has special cells that contain pigment (color). When these cells expand, the lizard's color is dark, but when the cells shrink, the lizard turns lighter.

The large eyes can swivel in separate directions, giving all-round vision.

HORNED LIZARD

Some lizards are covered with tough, spiky scales that help protect them from predators. Giant horned lizards also stay safe by hunting at dawn and dusk, and hiding beneath plants and rocks the rest of the time.

{ Fig 1: Horned lizards have rows of protective spines on their heads and backs. }

The body is covered with green-blue scaly skin. The back is humped.

A chameleon's tail is long and can coil around branches.

CAMOUFLAGE

Parson's chameleons are some of the most colorful lizards. They live in trees, where their green skin provides perfect camouflage.

79

AXOLOTL

THIS strange amphibian looks like a tadpole even when it is an adult. Such animals are called neotenous, and they can reproduce even though they have the bodies of young animals.

SENSING PREY

Axolotls are hunters, and they find their prey using eyesight and smell. They are also able to sense the electricity made in the muscles of another animal's body.

The wide skull is oval in shape. Behind it, cartilage stalks support gills that absorb oxygen from water for breathing.

Axolotls grow up to 8 inches long. They have smooth bodies and long, flat tails.

The mouth can open wide because the jaw hinges are set far back in the skull.

UNDER THREAT

These amphibians are a type of salamander that comes from Mexico. However, many of their natural habitats have been destroyed, and axolotls are now nearly extinct in the wild.

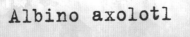

Albino axolotl

This captive axolotl is an albino, which means that it does not have its normal color pigment—melanin—that turns skin and eyes dark.

{ Fig 1: External gills }

EXTERNAL GILLS

Axolotls breathe using gills, which are on the outside of their bodies. This is normal in most young amphibians, but unusual in adults.

AXOLOTL LARVA

When an axolotl hatches from an egg, it is called a larva. It is about half an inch long and has no limbs. Its limbs will begin to grow when the larva is about 20 days old.

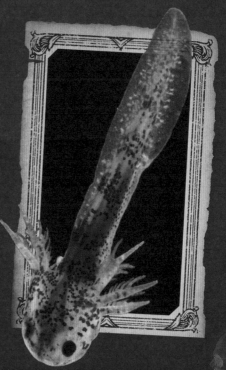

There are many small teeth. They are stumplike cones used to grip food.

AMPHIBIANS

AN AMPHIBIAN is an animal that leads two different lives. Young amphibians hatch in water and remain there till they are full grown. Most adults can live on land and in water. They return to water to lay eggs.

The forelimbs are used for gripping, and they are much shorter than the hind limbs, which are used for jumping and leaping.

SALAMANDER

Salamanders are types of amphibian with long bodies and tails. They can live on land or in the water, but they always prefer damp places.

LEAF FROGS

Tiger-striped leaf frogs have striped legs and orange bellies, and they climb rather than jump. They live in tropical forests where it rains most days. Leaf frogs avoid the harsh sun by hiding under leaves and hunting at night.

Frogs have smooth, moist skin that is often colorful.

FIRE-BELLIED TOAD

When a fire-bellied toad is scared, it rears up and shows off its bright orange or red color. It is also armed with a toxic skin that tastes nasty. Hungry predators tend to stay away from these amphibians!

{ Fig 1: Oriental fire-bellied toad }

Frogs have large eyes that roll backward when the animal swallows. This movement of the eyeballs helps food pass into the throat.

GREAT CRESTED NEWT LARVA

The larva of a great crested newt spends about four months in water before it is able to clamber out onto land. It will take another two to four years to reach adulthood.

SKIN PROTECTION

These frogs have smooth skin because they coat it in a waxlike substance to stop it from drying out. This substance also protects the skin from sunburn.

Common frog

Common frogs lay their eggs in ponds or slow-flowing rivers. Tadpoles emerge from the eggs and slowly develop into adult frogs. In the winter, common frogs hibernate to avoid freezing to death.

{ Fig 1: Common frogs leap to escape predators }

GOLIATH TIGERFISH

GOLIATH TIGERFISH are huge African predators with massive mouths and many daggerlike teeth. These fish live in waters and lakes, where they hunt other animals. Some have even been known to grab low-flying birds.

Powerful hunter

Tigerfish have long, lean bodies covered in silvery and colored scales. Their bodies are packed with muscles, giving them great strength for pursuing prey.

The skull is made of hardened bone. The lower jaw is sturdy enough to deliver a deadly bite.

HUNTER'S VISION

The large eyes partly face forward, allowing the fish to see its victim in front and watch for danger coming from the side.

DEADLY BITE

Goliath tigerfish are some of the fiercest freshwater fish in the world. Once they have found their victim, they swim in for the kill. They often hunt in groups. Their sharp teeth interlock to grab and slice their victim.

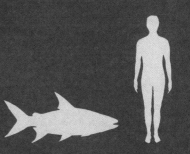

TOOTHY GRIN

The large, razor-sharp teeth are set right at the edge of the fish's jaws.

A goliath tigerfish can grow up to 5 feet long and weigh as much as a small adult human.

FRESHWATER FISH

FRESHWATER fish live in water that has very little dissolved salt in it. The very first fish lived in the sea, so freshwater fish have had to adapt to a different environment.

The dorsal fin runs the length of the fish's body.

CICHLIDS

There may be as many as 3,000 species of cichlids, and most of them live in Africa and South America.

The peacock cichlid has colorful, shimmering scales.

{ Fig 1: Pike }

∽ PIKE ∽

Northern pikes are powerful predators that live in lakes and rivers. They can grow to more than 3 ½ feet long. Pikes hunt other fish, even hunting young pikes when there is no other food available. They have slender heads with long lower jaws.

CATFISH

Catfish lurk in murky places near the bottoms of rivers or lakes. They use their feelers—called barbels—to find their way in the dark.

PIRANHA

Slow-flowing rivers of South America are home to piranha fish. They live and hunt in groups so they can attack animals that are bigger than them.

COLORFUL FISH

Male peacock cichlids have dazzling colors that shimmer in the light, but females are plain. Peacock cichlids hunt in dark water, but they can find prey using their lateral lines. These are organs on a fish's flanks (sides) that detect vibrations.

River lamprey

Lampreys do not have jaws or scales. They have long, eel-like bodies and strange sucker mouths that grip on to their prey. They can grow up to 16 inches in length.

HAMMERHEAD

HAMMERHEAD SHARKS
live throughout the world's oceans, especially in warm water close to land. A broad head helps a hammerhead shark swim and change direction quickly.

The skull grows out to the sides, creating the huge lobes on the shark's head. The eyes are positioned at the ends of the lobes.

The skull is made of cartilage, which is strong enough to protect the fish's brain, eyes, and snout, but also provides flexibility.

Different hammerheads

There are nine species of hammerhead. This is a scalloped hammerhead shark, which lives in very shallow water. It is one of the most common hammerhead species.

CARTILAGE
A shark doesn't have a bony skeleton. Instead, its skeleton is made of a bonelike material called cartilage. This is not quite as hard as ordinary bone, although it looks and feels similar.

SCHOOLING

Most hammerheads live alone, but young scalloped hammerheads sometimes gather in big groups called schools.

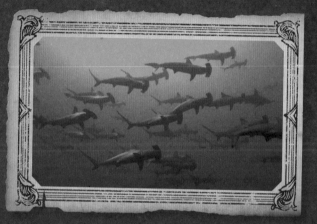

SCALLOPED EDGE

The front of a scalloped hammerhead's broad head has a curvy, "scalloped" edge.

This is the skull of a smooth hammerhead. Its mouth is huge and contains many rows of sharp teeth.

 Smooth hammerheads usually measure up to 10 feet long.

OCEAN FISH

FISH make up one of the largest and most diverse groups of animals on the planet. Most fish live in the sea and have tube-shaped, muscular bodies with gills for breathing and fins that aid swimming.

BASKING SHARK

Basking sharks are the second-largest fish in the world, after whale sharks. They feed on plankton—small living things that float in the ocean. As they swim, water pours into their mouths and over sievelike structures called gill rakers.

The basking shark has a huge body, with a skeleton of cartilage. It can grow up to 33 feet in length.

Barracuda

The long, silvery body of a barracuda shimmers under the sea. These predators often hunt in packs, speeding through the water in pursuit of their prey.

{ Fig 1: Basking shark teeth }

ANGLERFISH

Most fish, such as anglerfish, have skeletons made of bone, not cartilage. Anglerfish live in the deep sea where there is little or no light. They use a glowing light on the tip of a fishing rod above their heads to attract prey toward their mouths.

{ Fig 2: Anglerfish }

FILTER FEEDER

As water flows into a basking shark's mouth, plankton is caught on the gill rakers, while water flows out of the gill slits.

The snout is pointed and the mouth is vast. The teeth are tiny and not used in feeding. As the shark swims, it keeps its mouth open to gulp in food.

WOBBEGONG

Wobbegongs are strange-looking sharks with flat, patterned bodies. They live on the seabed, where their colors and frilled edges help to camouflage them.

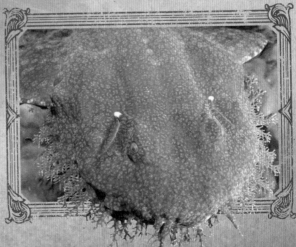

91

SKULL NAMES

Parietal bone

'THIS human head has been separated to show you the main bones that make up a human skull.

Occipital bone

Malleus (hammer)

Incus (anvil)

Stapes (stirrup)

Temporal bone

Zygomatic bone

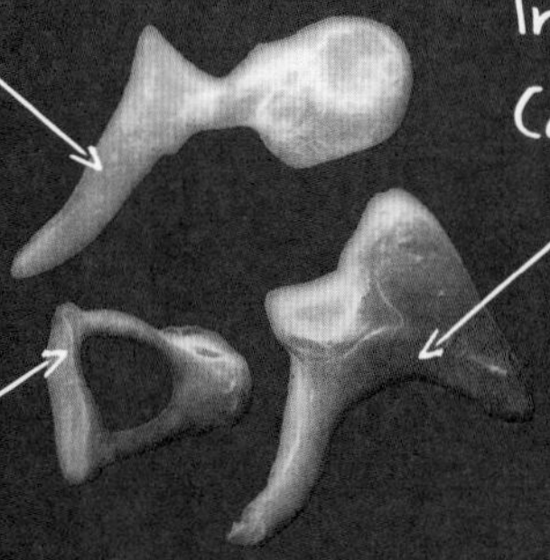

EAR BONES

The smallest bones in the human body are the three tiny bones in the ear (shown above, enlarged). Other mammals also have these bones, which carry vibrations to the inner ear. Scientists think that they evolved from the jawbones of our distant ancestors.

The mandible, or jaw bone, is attached to the skull with a flexible joint. This allows us to move our teeth forward, backward, and side-to-side.

Frontal bone

Maxilla

Maxilla

Incisors

Canine

Mandible

Molars

Premolars

Anteater

Curlew

TEETH

Humans have four different kinds of teeth. At the front are the incisors, which are used for slicing. Next to the incisors are the canines— strong teeth for tearing. Behind the canines are the premolars and molars, which are used for chewing.

GLOSSARY

AMPHIBIAN
An animal that can live on land and in water. Many amphibians start their lives as larvae living in water, then emerge onto land as adults.

BALEEN
Plates made of keratin inside the mouths of some whales, such as humpback whales and blue whales. The whales use the baleen plates to filter small fish and krill from the water.

BEAK
The hard mouthparts of a bird and some other animals, such as turtles. Birds' beaks come in many shapes, depending on their diet. Also called a bill.

BIRD
An animal with feathers whose front limbs are wings. Birds lay eggs and are warm-blooded, meaning that they keep their temperature constant.

BLOWHOLE
A hole at the top of the heads of whales and dolphins. The animals only breathe through their blowholes, not through their mouths.

CARRION
The bodies of dead animals that other animals eat. Many animals, such as hyenas, both hunt live prey and eat carrion. Others, such as vultures, just eat carrion.

CARTILAGE
A flexible substance found at the joints of bones, in the rib cage, and in our ears and noses. A shark's whole skeleton is made of cartilage.

ECHOLOCATION
A system of sounds produced by animals such as bats and dolphins to locate prey and find their way in the dark. Sounds bounce off an object, and the animal judges the object's position by listening to the echo.

FINS
Flaps on the sides and backs of fish, whales, and dolphins, which they use to swim.

FISH
Animals that live in water and breathe using gills. Fish use their fins and muscles attached to their backbones to move their bodies in an S shape.

FLIPPERS
Limbs of some aquatic animals that are used for swimming. In penguins, the wings have adapted to become flippers. In turtles and seals, the flippers are their modified arms and legs.

GILL
A body part in fish and some amphibians that allows them to breathe underwater. The gills take in oxygen that is dissolved in the water.

HIBERNATE
To go into a deep sleeplike state to survive the cold of winter. When animals hibernate, their bodies cool and their heart rate slows down to save energy.

HOOF
The horn-covered tip of the toes of some mammals, which they use to walk on. Sheep, deer, and pigs have two hooves on each foot, while horses and zebras have just one.

KERATIN
A tough protein that our hair and nails are made from. The scales, horns, shells, and hooves of many animals are also made of keratin.

MAMMALS
A group of warm-blooded animals that have hairy bodies. Female mammals produce milk from special glands and use it to feed their young.

MARSUPIALS
A group of mammals that give birth to very small young. The mothers then carry the young in a pouch while they grow. Marsupials include kangaroos, koalas, and opossums.

MUSCLE
A body part that can contract, or squeeze. Muscles are attached to bones and move them.

ORBIT
A socket in the skull that surrounds the eye. The orbit is formed from several bones, with the frontal bone at the top and the maxilla at the bottom.

PREENING
The smoothing and cleaning of feathers by birds. Their bodies produce a special oil to keep the feathers waterproof or in good condition for flying. Birds spread this oil using their beaks.

PRIMATES
A group of mammals that have large brains. Primates have hands or feet that can grasp and pick up objects. Monkeys, lemurs, chimpanzees, and humans are all primates.

RAPTOR
A bird of prey. Raptors have sharp talons, which they use to catch hold of prey, and hooked beaks, which they use to tear the prey apart.

REPTILES
A group of animals that have scaly skin and mostly lay eggs. Reptiles are cold-blooded, which means they cannot keep their body temperature constant. Crocodiles, turtles, snakes, and lizards are all reptiles.

SAGITTAL CREST
A ridge of bone that runs along the top of the skulls of many mammals and reptiles. The strong jaw muscles are attached to the sagittal crest.

SPECIES
A group of living things of the same type. Members of the same species are very similar to one another and can breed and produce offspring.

TADPOLE
The young of amphibians such as frogs and toads.

TALONS
The sharp, hooked claws of birds of prey, such as eagles, hawks, and owls. The birds use their talons to catch hold of prey.

TUSK
An enlarged tooth that sticks out of an animal's mouth. Elephants and walruses have two tusks in their upper jaws.

VENOM
A chemical produced in the bodies of some animals, such as snakes, which they inject into the blood of their victims using a bite or a sting. Once in the blood, the venom causes illness or death.

VERTEBRATE
An animal with a backbone. The backbone is a row of bones called vertebrae. Running through the vertebrae is a spinal cord, which is a bundle of nerves that carry messages between the brain and other parts of the body.

INDEX

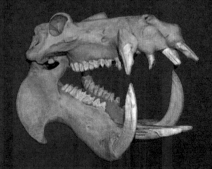